© 2024 Jayson Blondin
All rights reserved.

ISBN: 9798327147751
Published by Creative Synergy LLC

No part of this book may be reproduced, stored in a retrieval system, or transmitted in any form or by any means, electronic, mechanical, photocopying, recording, or otherwise, without the prior written permission of the publisher. Published by Creative Synergy LLC

Dedication

This book is dedicated to all the aspiring artists who dare to dream, but especially to my mother, who has always been there for me through every up and down. Your unwavering support and love have been my guiding light, and this book is a testament to your endless encouragement and belief in me. Thank you for being my rock and inspiration.

Acknowledgments

I would like to thank everyone who supported me on this journey, especially my family, friends, and mentors. Your encouragement and guidance made this book possible.

The Not So Starving Artist
The Business of Art

Table of Contents

1. Introduction
   The Myth of the Starving Artist
   My Journey Begins
2. Chapter 1: Embracing Your Passion
   Finding Your Artistic Voice
   My Early Artistic Influences
3. Chapter 2: Overcoming Financial Barriers
   Navigating Financial Challenges
   Staying Motivated Through Financial Struggles
4. Chapter 3: Developing a Business Mindset
   Turning Your Passion into a Viable Business
   Crafting Your Business Plan
5. Chapter 4: Building Your Client Base
   Finding and Expanding Your Audience
   Building Relationships with Clients
6. Chapter 5: Forming Strategic Partnerships
   The Power of Collaboration
   Benefits of Strategic Partnerships
7. Chapter 6: Marketing and Expanding Your Reach
   The Importance of Effective Marketing
   Leveraging Social Media
8. Chapter 7: Innovative Business Models
   Diversifying Your Income
   Developing Niche Markets
9. Chapter 8: Handling Setbacks and Failures
   Embracing Failure as a Catalyst for Success
   Strategies for Overcoming Setbacks
10. Chapter 9: Scaling Your Business
    Transitioning from Local to National (or Global) Reach

                Leveraging Technology
11.   Chapter 10: Achieving Long-term Success
                Sustaining Your Success
                Building Strong Client Relationships
12.   Chapter 11: Planning for Continued Growth and Success
                Vision for the Future
                Setting Long-term Goals
13.   Chapter 12: Conclusion and Final Thoughts
                Reflecting on the Journey
                Words of Encouragement
                Acknowledgments

Introduction to the Author and Book

Welcome to "The Not So Starving Artist," a guide designed to help you navigate the challenges and triumphs of starting and running a successful art business. I'm Jayson Blondin, and I wrote this book to share my journey and to help aspiring artists break free from the myth of the "starving artist."

Like many of you, I faced countless obstacles and setbacks on my path to becoming a full-time artist. From financial hurdles to personal missteps, my journey was anything but smooth. However, through perseverance, creativity, and a strategic approach, I turned my passion for art into a thriving business.

In this book, you'll find practical advice, personal anecdotes, and step-by-step strategies to help you build your own successful art career. Whether you're just starting out or looking to take your existing business to the next level, "The Not So Starving Artist" is here to guide you every step of the way. But first, here is my story in a nutshell:

The Myth of the Starving Artist

Let me start by saying this book is not about getting rich quick. I'm not going to pretend that you will become a millionaire overnight. However, what I can promise is that you will gain the tools and business mindset that, when combined with your artistic talent, will enable you to run your own lucrative art business and support yourself doing what you love. To put things into perspective, my best year brought in $90,000. I'm immensely proud of this achievement, especially since I built this business entirely on my own. Every piece of artwork that generated that $90,000 was touched by my hands. This book will show you how to achieve your own success and turn your passion for art into a sustainable career.

The idea of the "starving artist" has long been a part of our cultural consciousness, but it doesn't have to be your reality. This book is about transforming your passion for art into a sustainable, thriving business. I'll share my personal journey, from struggling with financial barriers to achieving long-term success, and provide actionable steps to help you do the same.

My Journey Begins

My journey started with a deep passion for art and a determination to make it my career, despite the odds. I faced significant challenges, like being accepted to Ringling College of Art and Design but unable to attend due to financial constraints. These experiences shaped my path and fueled my drive to succeed.

I believe in order to start something, you need to just get started. You might fail, but who cares? Not trying is just another form of failure. Like Edison, who famously said, '*I have not failed. I've just found 10,000 ways that won't work*,' you can fail a thousand times, but it only takes getting it right once to succeed.

No one was going to do this for me, and I was hungry to start. I had been accepted to Ringling College of Art and Design, the number one school for animation in the world, where Disney handpicked artists from, and I was so excited, but I couldn't afford it, even with a full scholarship. It was a private college, and their full scholarship did not cover everything. Then, the program was so intensive that they would not allow the students to work a job. So, I was not able to make it happen, no matter how dedicated I was.

This almost broke me, but it fueled me to try something new. I was determined. At the time, I was working part-time in a restaurant and also doing murals and commissions here and there. It was nice, but if I wanted to do only art for a living, then I had to make more money as an artist so that I could survive doing only what I love. I knew I had to create a body of work and I knew I needed a client base. These things take time, but I was in a rush. An artist friend told me that I should not do portraits for a living, which I loved doing, because there is not enough money in it, but I have always been stubborn and I only wanted to prove him wrong and do it more now. I knew there was a way to take a business mindset to the equation and make it happen. This would be the "business of art," and I knew that most artists don't think this way. But I was not normal and wanted to do things differently.

The first thing I noticed when I wanted to start my business is how hard it was for an artist to get started. The cliché of "the starving artist" is a real thing and it's hard to get paid. The first thing I noticed was family and friends were not good clientele. Everyone wanted something for a discount if not for free. I had to get out of this circle and into one who had money and wanted to spend it.

I knew that I could not just create art that I love, but, I should instead cater my art to what the client wants. Make it a service and become an artist for hire. The first thing I did was make a decision to try to find a way to expand my reach and create a business.

I think this step might be different for everyone, but for me, my first thought was to find a business partner that might complement my artistic skills. I wanted to do portraits. I was really good at portraits and I wanted to create custom portraits for people. I was intrigued by the old Renaissance artists that would do commissions for the wealthy.

I had this idea for "life portraits" for graduating high school seniors. It would be a way to highlight their momentous occasions while highlighting their wants, desires, passions, and where they wanted to go in life.

I had already made one. And now I just needed a way to expand and market and turn it into a business. I had this idea that if I wanted to do this, I needed to partner with someone who had the eyes and ears of the clients I wanted, and I had an old high school friend who was a photographer and I thought this would be perfect. We had a great relationship and rapport. We worked very well together. This was perfect.

I contacted her and we hit it off with ideas and had the idea to start an LLC. She would keep her photography business and we would have a joint LLC for the art side of things. We eventually got involved with a few high schools and we were so excited that we decided to move the business to another state. We thought a state with a booming economy would be smart, so, we chose Texas. We were living in Florida at the time. Plus, I had a cousin in Texas, so I wasn't completely alone. This made sense and was risky enough but with a very slight safety net just in case.

We created our LLC. We decided on "Creative Synergy LLC" because it left us room to have many different types of businesses under this umbrella. Had we chosen something specific like "Portraits LLC" then we would be forced to stick with just this, so we wanted to leave room for future growth.

I spent the next year driving back and forth from Florida to Texas. We found a nice location in the city of Deep Ellum to build a studio. Our plan was to start small. We would build the studio with an apartment on top so I could live there. And she would live on her own with her boyfriend. We signed all of the papers, and we designed the studio with the landlord and we even finished the floors and put our logo in the floor. Things were moving great. Our own art and photography studio was on it's way!

In order to make the move to Texas, I sold everything that I owned. Even sold my car. I was all in and determined to do whatever it took. I was living the life and this was an exciting time. We weren't making much but we knew we could expand and make this happen. We were both educated, talented, and determined. And with her photography business, in conjunction with our collaborated art business with me as the artist, we saw no way to fail. The only way to go was up. We would do our "life portraits" as well as her photography, as well as murals, and custom art commissions.

Now, this part of the story is where I say that you need to be prepared for hiccups, road bumps, and failures. Because, just before the build was finished, I completely fell flat on my face and almost lost everything.

One night while in Texas, she and I were finishing the floors, and I did probably the most idiotic thing I could have done. I couldn't help the urges I had and I poured my heart out and confessed my love for her. I told her that I was in love with her. Boy, was I a fool. She was obviously in love with her boyfriend. But, I couldn't help but be honest. This was the start of our demise. We stayed friends, of course, but now things were awkward, and little by little things fell apart. We decided to part ways. And I bought her out of my LLC that I designed, and we eventually got out of our contract with the landlord. It was really heartbreaking. I knew I had ruined my dreams. Or so I thought. It turns out that failure can be an amazing catalyst for success when harnessed properly.

Most people would quit here. I almost went back home, all beat up and defeated. But something inside me wouldn't let me quit. While I was really upset, I became more determined. I was embarrassed for sure. So, here I was, in an entirely new state. I was away from my family. I was temporarily living at my cousin's house until the studio was finished being built. And now that was not happening. So, I picked myself up off the floor and made a new way. I got a job as a server because I needed to make some money. I got myself an apartment with my first paycheck. I worked doubles for 3-4 days a week and had the other half of the week off. So I was able to put in 40 hours at the restaurant and 40 hours into my business. All of my free time was surrounded by starting my business. I knew that I had to work harder than everyone else and I had to sacrifice in order to get something new. I had this idea of it being like a hand of cards in poker. Maybe you don't have anything in your hand. And no matter how many times or ways you move or rearrange the cards around, there was no way to make a good hand. So, the only thing you can do is add some new cards by discarding what didn't work and grabbing a few new cards. So, I studied, and I read, and I researched, and I made art. I was painting canvases of what I really enjoyed, trying to build a body of work, and I was starting a website to showcase these. I was learning how to use social media for my benefit and learning how to market using social media, which at the time was a fairly new concept.

After 6 months of working in the restaurant, I was able to quit and work solely for myself. And I am going to show you exactly how I did it.

I was doing some commissions and murals here and there. And commissions alone, without a large reach would not be sustainable. I needed to grow first. But, I didn't have any real sales on my website yet. I wasn't making much, but I was able to work as only an artist. This was a huge success to me. I was living the dream. My bills were paid, but I was broke. So I had to adjust and create some residual income by broadening my revenue streams.

I knew Texans liked their wine, their dogs, and art. So, this was my focus. At the time, painting parties were a fairly new thing, but since I don't like doing what everyone else is doing, I tried to think of a new way. I had this idea of painting on wine glasses. I didn't have my own studio space. I couldn't afford this. I was barely making my rent at my apartment. So, I tried to think of a way to have my own painting parties with wine glasses instead of on canvas.

The first step was getting a few designs under my belt. So I scoured the internet for inspiration. I made my focus on having a few designs for each season or holiday throughout the year. I also made a few sports-themed glasses, because Texas also loves their sports, and I was a huge cowboy fan. I started an Etsy store, linked it with my website and social media, and little by little added my glasses to the site. I found wine glasses that were great, super thick and cheap, from the dollar store. My glasses would only cost $1! Then the glass paint I needed was in the craft section of Michael's. Also, not expensive. Then, the brushes, also from Michael's, were cheap, watercolor brushes. I found these worked the best on glass. All I needed was a setup for a party. I needed water cups, tablecloths, brushes, glasses, paint plates, paint, and some designs. I was on my way. I used simple styrofoam party plates for the paint, and easy, cheap, plastic disposable cups for the water along with dollar tree tablecloths. So all of my material would be from dollar tree and Michael's. So, it cost me less than $5 per person to have a setup with all of my materials. Not bad; not bad at all. The rest of my cost was just my time and effort. I then came up with an offshoot for my LLC to market wine glasses, and I made a new logo just for this part of the business. I kept it all in the same theme as my main logo though. This is important. You want everything to flow together. Everything should all look like one big happy family, even though the children might be a little different.

Eventually, I now needed a way to host the parties. I knew I didn't have my own space. I couldn't afford to rent my apartment and rent a studio space at the same time. And I didn't have the clientele to advertise to get any parties either. So, I had the idea of partnering with local businesses to pull this off. The way I figured it, if each person was paying a price to come and paint, this cost would have to cover all of the expenses and leave extra for me to make a profit. I did research as to what the painting with a twist was charging and went from there. I contacted a few wine bars and asked if they'd be interested in hosting a party once a month at their venue. They would market to their clients. I would also share on my social media, and we would charge a certain amount and they would get a percentage of every ticket sold and I would get the remainder. We agreed on charging $35 per person. I would get $25 and they would get $10, and they would pay for materials. So, I went to each bar and spoke with the owners. My first bar was a success. The owner loved the idea, and my business was birthed. We agreed on a first design. It was October, so my first glass was a Halloween-themed glass with a cute ghost on it, and it said: "I'm here for the boos" on the side. They immediately started marketing the party and taking orders for tickets. Within a week, we had over 40 people signed up! I couldn't believe it, I was shocked! And, very excited. So, I spent the next few weeks getting all of my materials. I needed a bag on wheels to carry all of my art supplies. I needed brushes for each person, enough cups, enough plates, tablecloths, paper towels and glasses. I also needed all of the paints.

The night of the party, I was so nervous. I was about to walk 45 women at a wine bar through how to paint my wine glass design, while they were drinking. What was I thinking!? I had never done anything like this before and I was so nervous, it wasn't even funny. I got to the bar and realized I had no idea what to do. The owner helped me get started with setting up tables. We knew where everyone was sitting. So I put down tablecloths and water cups, brushes, and paper towels at each seat. People started filling in and I waited to put paint on the plates so that the paint wouldn't dry. I put a dab of each color paint needed for the design on each plate, and placed a plate at each seat. I set myself up with a setup as well so I could paint with them and guide them through the process. Music was playing and the energy in the room was intense. The bar was filled to the brim with women, all drinking and talking, and ready for a great night. I was freaking out. Finally, the owner lowered the music and made an announcement from behind the bar introducing me. This was it. Then, it was my turn to take over and talk. You could hear a pin drop. What did I get myself into?

I finally started talking. I introduced myself and explained how everything would go, and since I was behind the bar, I asked them to raise their hands if they needed any help, and told them I would rush over. I projected my voice and began… I raised my wine glass and started with painting the first step. I had already practiced at home and knew each step-by-step process. I guided them step-by-step to completion. For the next two hours, I was running all over the bar, making sure to speak with and tend to each person and each group. I took pictures of everyone individually as well as groups as the painting progressed. I knew I could use these images afterward to post on social media. I had a new iPhone and I was excited to test the new camera. Some posed and some were shots of them simply painting. We had a blast and I met so many people. I invited all of them to send me a friend request on Facebook so they could get their pictures. I told them they could tag themselves. This was my way of building a client list. Yes, I had a business Facebook page, but I was wanting to have friends first. The relationship was important for my small business. Also, i knew that once they left the bar, the chances of them going to my business page was minimal. Life happens and people forget. This method worked. They would all eventually send me a request and tag themselves, and share my photos, even before they left the bar. And I still invited all of them via Facebook to my business page once i got home, and I now had them twice, on my personal Facebook, and my business Facebook; which would also trickle to my Instagram. In the end, I walked out of that bar, after two hours of running around like a madman, with a check for $1,125. I was elated to say the least. The party was a huge success. This business model had been proven. The bar made money and so did I. And the clients were over the moon happy with their glasses. Everyone left with something they were proud of, and they were all buzzing about me with their friends and family and all over social media. I was being tagged left and right. People were even wanting to take pictures with me.

 The bar owner couldn't wait to set another date. We scheduled the next month's party. The next one filled up so fast, that we had to do a second one the following night for the overflow. I was basically doing 2 parties a month at this one location. And making great money. Now, I just needed more bars to add to the family. The ladies would come every month to see the new glass designs. Every month was a new design. We had designs for the whole year and for every occasion and holiday. Eventually, I was doing these at wine bars as well as at vineyards and country clubs, and with classes with upwards of 80 people!

The next big thing that happened is that through this process I was meeting so many people. These ladies fell in love with me at the parties. I was booking private parties in homes for all sorts of occasions and for birthdays. And I was also getting extra commissions in the process because I shared my work with everyone at the parties, so I was making money from every angle. Pet portraits was one of the angles I was pushing and I was getting a ton of commissions for these. Before I knew it, I was making over $5,000 a month and only working like 3 days a month, not counting my studio time in my apartment working on commissions my website and social media. One night, I met a new business owner at one of my parties that just happened to own the pet boutique next door. We got to talking about parties at her place, but, instead of wine glasses, it would be pet portrait painting parties. All I had to do was figure out how to actually do this. I researched what I could, and came up with a plan. The model would be similar but instead of $35 per person for the glasses, these would be $50 per person. She could only fit 20 people in her boutique, so this was our max. One party each month, and she would market to her customers and I would market to mine. She would pay for materials as well. I would get $40 per person and she would get $10. The customers would send in a photo of their dog and I would sketch them on their canvases before the party, and I would show up with the canvases and guide each person through painting their own pet portraits. They loved me, and more importantly, they loved their portraits. They were proud of their own work and hung them up. I left each party with a check for $800. And each time I got new friends on Facebook who also followed me on my business page, and they would also order custom commissions from me. Especially my pet portraits I would do in oil. These would fetch me over $1,000 a pop. I was living my dream.

Eventually, I met my wife at one of my parties. I got married, and built my own studio onto our home and would continue working as an artist for the next decade until retirement. I kept adding to my art options. I was doing a ton of parties all over the tri-county area, both wine glasses and pet, and a ton of private parties in homes, where I didn't have to share the profits with anyone. I was doing custom oil commissions and murals, and even live-wedding paintings. I loved these the most. For a 6-8 hour length of time at a wedding painting live, I would make upwards of $2,000-$5,000. Plus I was shipping my custom glasses all over the country.

And all of this was possible because I blended the concepts of business with my dream of becoming an artist. I broke the barriers to the concepts of a starving artist. I was not so starving. This is possible for anyone and I believe that this model can be replicated for anyone who wants to start out on their own. I had no help and was doing everything myself, marketing, website design, logo… I taught myself how to do everything one at a time. We live in an age where there is an over abundance of knowledge available online if one is only willing to take the time to look. I risked all and sacrificed my time to make my dreams a reality. If I hadn't taken the leap of moving to a new state away from family and all distractions, and being completely on my own in the middle of the deep ocean that was utterly terrifying, I might not have ever swam to the other end of the pool to my success. I failed countless times and each failure set me up for a future success. By not focusing on what I lacked, but using what I lacked to my advantage, such as utilizing other businesses to host my parties, I was able to market and build a huge client base that has lasted for over a decade and is still growing, and all with a very low overhead cost. I now am retired and I travel the country doing live-wedding paintings, and I still do private parties every now and then, but for a much higher charge. And I still do custom commissions as well. But I am also working on a novel and a children's book. This has led me down a path of following and achieving every dream I ever had. And, yes, you can do this too.

Get out of your comfort zone. Dive into the deep end. Risk everything. Lose everything. And once you have nothing left to lose, then that is when it starts. Think outside of the box. Look at things from every angle. Learn to use social media as a tool for your business instead of being a tool for their gain. Meet people. Learn how to communicate with others. Learn how to promote yourself. Learn how to fail. Learn new things. Don't just stick to doing only what you love for art. Consider yourself as a service; and artist for hire. Every time a client wants something, say, yes. Then figure out how to do it. Research what you should charge. Research how your process should look. If you fail, who cares. You might meet your future wife or husband in the process, or the next big client willing to pay some huge amount of money for something that might be easy for you to do, but not so easy for someone else. Follow your heart and chase your dreams. Never give up, even when it seems all is lost. But you have to shuffle some new cards into your hand if you want to play a different outcome. And always remember; things don't get better by chance, they get better with change.

The Myth of the Starving Artist continued...

For far too long, the notion of the "starving artist" has held back countless talented individuals from pursuing their dreams. This outdated stereotype suggests that making a living from art is nearly impossible, and that artists must sacrifice financial stability for their passion. It's time to debunk this myth.

Artists can and do make a living from their work. It requires a blend of creativity and business acumen, but it's entirely possible. By adopting a business mindset and leveraging the right strategies, you can create a sustainable and profitable art career.

What You'll Learn

In "The Not So Starving Artist," we'll cover everything you need to know to succeed as an artist in today's world. Here's a brief overview of what you'll find in each chapter:

1. Getting Started: Embracing failure and taking the first step.
2. Overcoming Financial Barriers: Navigating financial challenges and staying motivated.
3. Developing a Business Mindset: Turning your passion into a viable business.
4. Building Your Client Base: Finding and expanding your audience.
5. Forming Strategic Partnerships: Collaborating for success.
6. Marketing and Expanding Your Reach: Effective marketing strategies and building an online presence.
7. Innovative Business Models: Creating unique offerings and adapting to trends.
8. Handling Setbacks and Failures: Turning failures into opportunities.
9. Scaling Your Business: Growing and diversifying your art business.
10. Achieving Long-term Success: Sustaining and evolving your business over the long term.

So, let's dive in and start this journey together. It's time to prove that the starving artist is a thing of the past. Your dream of a successful art career is within reach, and this book will show you how to achieve it.

Chapter 1: Getting Started

The Importance of Taking the First Step

Starting an art business can be daunting. The fear of failure often holds many back, but the truth is, not trying is the only real failure. Embracing the possibility of failure is the first step towards success. As Thomas Edison famously said about inventing the lightbulb, "I have not failed. I've just found 10,000 ways that won't work." It only takes one time of getting it right to succeed.

Taking the first step requires courage and a willingness to embrace uncertainty. Many aspiring artists hesitate, fearing they are not ready or that they will make mistakes. However, it's important to remember that every successful artist started somewhere. The key is to begin, learn, and adapt. Learn to love problems. It's within problems that the best solutions lay hidden, just waiting to be found.

Embracing Failure as a Learning Opportunity

Failure is not the end; it's a valuable teacher. Each misstep is an opportunity to learn and grow. When I was first accepted to Ringling College of Art and Design, I was ecstatic. It was the number one school for animation, and I had a full scholarship. However, the costs beyond the scholarship and the intensive program that didn't allow for part-time work meant I couldn't afford to attend. This setback almost broke me, but it also fueled my determination to find another way to succeed.

Every failure teaches you something about your process, your market, and yourself. For example, not being able to attend Ringling taught me to seek alternative paths and to be resourceful. I learned to value resilience and creativity in overcoming obstacles.

My Initial Steps

At the time, I was working part-time in a restaurant and taking on mural and commission projects. It was nice, but I wanted to make a living solely from my art. I needed to create a body of work and build a client base, and I was in a rush to do so. An artist friend advised me against doing portraits for a living, citing a lack of profitability. However, my stubborn nature made me more determined to prove him wrong. I strongly believed in the idea of combining a business mindset with my artistic skills, something many artists overlook. Armed with my service mindset from working in hospitality, I knew that people love to spend money. If I could just provide a service that people wanted to pay for, everything would work out. I needed to find a market. I needed to find a hole to fill, so to speak.

My initial steps involved balancing multiple roles. Working in a restaurant provided a steady income and a flexible schedule, while my mural and commission projects helped build my portfolio. This dual approach allowed me to gradually transition into a full-time artist.

Determination and Drive

The first thing I noticed when I wanted to start my business was how hard it was for an artist to get started. The cliché of the "starving artist" is real; it's challenging to get paid for your work. Family and friends were not reliable clients—they wanted discounts or free work. I had to move beyond this circle and find clients who valued and could afford my work.

I realized I couldn't just create art that I loved; I needed to cater to what clients wanted and make my art a service. This required a business mindset and strategic thinking. I knew I had to expand my reach and create a business model that would work.

I began by researching my market. What types of art were in demand? Who were the potential clients? How could I differentiate my work from others? These questions guided my initial business strategy.

Taking the Leap

My first major step was deciding to find a business partner to complement my artistic skills. I wanted to focus on portraits, inspired by the old Renaissance artists who did commissions for the wealthy. I envisioned a concept called "life portraits" for high school seniors, capturing their passions and future aspirations during such a momentum time in their lives. To me, this was something I could market to a specific niche that was still in my realm of portraits and allowed me room for customizations and creativity. I had already made one and just needed a way to expand my reach and market it.

I contacted an old high school friend who was a photographer, and we hit it off with our ideas. I thought a photographer already had the eyes and ears of the exact clients I was hoping to market to. We decided to start an LLC together, named "Creative Synergy LLC," to allow for various types of art-related businesses under one umbrella. We wanted to leave room for future growth. We eventually moved our business to Texas, where we believed a booming economy would support our growth. Despite initial success, as I shared in my story, our partnership faced challenges, and we parted ways. This setback was devastating, but it also became a catalyst for my ultimate success.

Working with a partner initially helped me to leverage combined resources and skills. However, it also taught me the importance of clear communication and alignment of goals. Our partnership's end was a significant setback, but it also spurred me to take full control of my business direction.

Embracing Change and Moving Forward

I found myself in a new state, away from family, and temporarily living with a cousin. I felt completely alone. I picked myself up, got a job as a server to make ends meet, and dedicated all my free time to my art business. I knew I had to work harder and sacrifice more to achieve my dreams.

I built a body of work, created a website, and learned how to use social media for marketing. After six months of balancing a job and my art, I was able to quit the restaurant and focus entirely on my art business. This was a significant milestone and the beginning of my journey as a full-time artist.

During this period, I made significant sacrifices, including selling my car and living with minimal comforts. These sacrifices were necessary to invest more time and resources into my art. The determination to succeed despite the odds kept me motivated.

Conclusion of Chapter 1

Getting started is the hardest part, but it's also the most crucial. Embrace failure, learn from it, and keep moving forward. Your journey may not be smooth, but every step, no matter how difficult, brings you closer to your dream. In the next chapter, we'll delve into overcoming financial barriers and staying motivated despite the challenges.

Chapter 2: Overcoming Financial Barriers

Navigating Financial Challenges

One of the biggest obstacles aspiring artists face is the financial challenge of supporting themselves while pursuing their passion. When I was accepted to Ringling College of Art and Design, the reality of high tuition costs, even with a full scholarship, was a harsh wake-up call. Private colleges often come with hidden costs that scholarships don't cover, such as supplies, living expenses, and fees. Additionally, the rigorous program meant that students were not allowed to work part-time jobs, further complicating the financial equation.

This financial barrier nearly crushed my dreams, but it also pushed me to think creatively about alternative paths. It's important to recognize that while financial challenges are real, they are not insurmountable. Here are some strategies I used to overcome these barriers, which can help you too:

- Budgeting: Track your expenses meticulously and identify areas where you can cut costs. This might mean living more frugally than you're accustomed to, but every dollar saved is a dollar you can invest in your art.
- Finding Part-Time Work: Look for jobs that offer flexible hours and won't drain your creative energy. Working in a restaurant, for example, allowed me to make ends meet while still having time to work on my art.
- Alternative Education: If traditional college is financially out of reach, consider other forms of education

such as online courses, workshops, and mentorships. These can be more affordable and equally effective.

Staying Motivated Through Financial Struggles

Staying motivated when financial struggles are weighing you down is challenging, but it's crucial for long-term success. When I faced the financial reality of not being able to attend my dream college, I had to find ways to keep my motivation high. Here's what helped me, and what can help you too:

- Set Clear Goals: Define what success looks like for you and set short-term and long-term goals. Having a clear vision of what you want to achieve can keep you focused and driven. One of the motivators that helped we was seeing other artists that were doing there art for a living. It pushed me to believe it's possible.
- Celebrate Small Wins: Acknowledge and celebrate small victories along the way. Whether it's completing a project, making a sale, or learning a new skill, recognizing these achievements can boost your morale. Even better, share them on your social media so your followers can share in the success with you. They love to hear your good news just as much as you do. And people like to give money to people who make money. It's weird but it works. There mind will be focused on what they could purchase from you, and this is a great place for a potential client to be.
- Surround Yourself with Supportive People: Build a network of friends, family, and fellow artists who support and encourage you. Their belief in you can help sustain your motivation during tough times.

Creating Multiple Income Streams

One of the key lessons I learned early on is the importance of diversifying your income streams. Relying solely on one source of income can not only be risky, but also not smart, especially in the unpredictable world of art. Here's how I created multiple income streams to support myself:

- Commissions and Murals: In addition to my part-time job, I took on mural projects and commissions. This not only provided extra income but also helped build my portfolio.
- Teaching Art Classes: Teaching art classes or workshops can be a great way to earn money while sharing your skills and passion with others. It also helps you build a local network and reputation.
- Selling Prints and Merchandise: Create and sell prints of your work, as well as merchandise like t-shirts, mugs, and phone cases. Your artwork can look great on many different household items. Walk through any home store and you'll see what I mean. This allows you to reach a wider audience and generate passive income.

Developing a Financial Plan

Having a solid financial plan is essential for turning your passion into a sustainable business. Here's how you can create one:

- Calculate Your Costs: List all your expenses, including supplies, studio rent, marketing, and living expenses. This will give you a clear picture of how much you need to earn.
- Set Income Goals: Based on your costs, set realistic income goals. Determine how many pieces you need to sell, how many commissions you need to book, or

how many classes you need to teach to meet your financial needs.
- Create a Pricing Strategy: Research the market to determine competitive pricing for your work. Factor in the cost of materials, your time, and the value of your artistic skills.

Overcoming Financial Barriers: Real-Life Examples

To give you a clearer picture of how to overcome financial barriers, here are a few real-life examples from my journey:

- The Power of Networking: I leveraged connections with other artists and local businesses to find opportunities. For example, partnering with a photographer friend helped us combine resources and reach a broader audience. And partnering with wine bars allowed me to save on renting studio space as well as increase my reach piggy backing off of their already established clientele.
- Crowdfunding and Grants: Consider exploring crowdfunding platforms like Kickstarter or applying for art grants. These can provide significant financial support for your projects.
- Bartering Services: Offer to exchange your art services for other services you need. For instance, I traded murals for free marketing services from a local business, which helped me grow my client base.

Conclusion of Chapter 2

Financial barriers are a significant challenge for many artists, but with determination, creativity, and strategic planning, they can be overcome. By budgeting wisely, creating multiple income streams, and developing a solid financial plan, you can turn your passion for art into a sustainable business. In the next chapter, we'll explore how to develop a business mindset and transform your artistic skills into a viable business.

Chapter 3: Developing a Business Mindset

Turning Your Passion into a Viable Business

For many artists, the idea of turning their passion into a business can seem daunting. Art is often seen as a purely creative endeavor, but to make a living from it, you need to approach it with a business mindset. This doesn't mean sacrificing your artistic integrity; rather, it involves finding a balance between creativity and practicality.

One of the first steps in developing a business mindset is recognizing that your art has value. This might seem obvious, but many artists struggle with pricing their work appropriately. Your time, skills, and creativity are worth something, and you should be compensated fairly for them.

Understanding the Basics of Business

Before diving into the specifics of running an art business, it's important to understand some basic business principles:

- Supply and Demand: Understand the market demand for your type of art. Research what buyers are looking for and how much they are willing to pay. Literally call other business if you have to. Reach out to other artists. Whatever you have to do.
- Pricing Strategies: Develop a pricing strategy that covers your costs and provides a profit. Consider

factors like materials, time, market rates, and the uniqueness of your work.
- Marketing and Branding: Learn how to market yourself and your art. This includes creating a brand, building a website, and using social media effectively. And communication is huge. Don't be shy. If your confident about your art, then they will be confident in you and your art as well. Customers are paying for your personality as much as they are your art. Put yourself out there with your best foot forward.
- Sales and Distribution: Explore different sales channels, such as galleries, online platforms, art fairs, and direct commissions. Even local businesses. They need art done all of the time and love to work with local artists.

Crafting Your Business Plan

A business plan is a roadmap for your art business. It outlines your goals, strategies, and the steps you'll take to achieve them. Here's a simple structure for creating your business plan:

- Executive Summary: A brief overview of your business, including your mission statement and what you hope to achieve.
- Market Analysis: Research on your target market, including potential customers and competitors.
- Marketing Strategy: How you plan to promote and sell your art. This could include social media marketing, collaborations, and exhibitions.
- Financial Plan: Your budget, pricing strategy, and financial goals. Include projections for income and expenses.

•   Operations Plan: The day-to-day operations of your business, including production schedules, suppliers, and logistics.

Building Your Brand

Your brand is how you present yourself and your art to the world. It's what sets you apart from other artists and makes you recognizable. Here are some key elements of building a strong brand:

•   Consistency: Use consistent visuals and messaging across all your platforms, including your website, social media, and promotional materials. Literally design a logo, then created multiple versions of your logo for different platforms and services you offer.
•   Authenticity: Be true to yourself and your artistic vision. Your brand should reflect your personality and values. This is where you can let your personality shine. It might be the fist thing you future client sees. This will be worth your tie learning how to create yourself as I did. And if not, you should pay another artist for this. It will be worth it. Trust me.
•   Storytelling: Share the story behind your art. This one is huge. People are often interested in the inspiration and process behind your work. They don't just want to buy art, they want to feel like they personally know the artist their buying from. Spend some good time writing down your personal story. The good, bad and ugly. They will love your honesty and will be more inclined to buy something simply because you made an impression on them. Look up what an 'Elevator pitch" is, and, know yours. Be ready to tell your story at anytime.
•   Professionalism: Present yourself as a professional artist. This includes having a well-designed

website, professional email address, professional email signature and high-quality images of your work. These days, this can easily be done with a new smart phone.

Leveraging Social Media

Social media is a powerful tool for artists. It allows you to reach a global audience, connect with other artists, and promote your work. Here are some tips for using social media effectively:

- Choose the Right Platforms: Focus on platforms where your target audience is most active. Instagram, Facebook, and Pinterest are popular choices for artists. I put myself on all of them. And Etsy is great once you have something to sell.
- Engage with Your Audience: Post regularly and often and interact with your followers. Respond to comments, participate in discussions, and show appreciation for your supporters. Don't just show them your finished work, but show them behind the scenes; your process. Show them what you do while your paint is drying on the canvas. Show your daily life of being an artist; the mundane and whimsical. They love this… then they will be primed to react well once you share a finished product of yours because they have been watching you create this from the beginning. They will feel invested.
- Show Your Process: Share behind-the-scenes content that gives people a glimpse into your creative process. This can include work-in-progress shots, studio tours, and time-lapse videos.
- Collaborate with Others: Partner with other artists, brands, or influencers to expand your reach. Collaborations can introduce your work to new audiences and create exciting opportunities.

Networking and Building Relationships

Building relationships is crucial for any business, and the art world is no exception. Networking can lead to collaborations, sales, and valuable insights. Here's how to build a strong network:

- Attend Events: Go to art shows, exhibitions, and industry events. These are great opportunities to meet other artists, gallery owners, and potential clients. Sign up for local art contests. Who cares if you don't win, you'll be able to meet people form your local area that might be able to tremendously help you.
- Join Online Communities: Participate in online forums, social media groups, and artist networks. These communities can provide support, feedback, inspiration and new opportunities. Do not underestimate the power of surrounding yourself with what you aspire to become.
- Follow Up: After meeting someone, follow up with a message or email. Keep in touch and build genuine relationships, not just business contacts. People will ever remember what you say or do, but they will always remember how you make them feel.

Staying Organized and Efficient

Running a business requires organization and efficiency. Here are some tips to help you stay on top of things:

- Use Project Management Tools: Tools like Trello, Asana, or Monday can help you manage projects, deadlines, and tasks. And apps for social media management are also highly advisable, such as Hootsuite. This has many useful functions and supports scheduling posts across multiple platforms, including Facebook, Twitter, Instagram, LinkedIn, and more.

• Keep Financial Records: Maintain detailed records of your income, expenses, and invoices. This will make tax time easier and help you track your financial health. And, as a small business owner with an LLC you will be able to write off everything business related, such as travel expenses, electronics, even your home space that you use to make art, and much more.

• Set a Schedule: Create a schedule that balances your creative time with business tasks. This can help you stay productive and avoid burnout. I put in a ton of hours, but I also made time for me to do whatever I wanted. Don't deprive yourself of creative time, or down time. It's crucial in avoiding burnout.

• Outsource When Necessary: Don't be afraid to delegate tasks that you're not good at or that take up too much time. This could include accounting, marketing, social media management or website maintenance. Sometimes it's better to spend a little money instead of your precious time. Consider the pros and cons of this first.

Exploring Additional Revenue Streams

In addition to selling original art, consider exploring other revenue streams to diversify your income:

• Prints and Reproductions: Offer high-quality prints of your work. This allows you to reach a broader audience and provide more affordable options. Their are many ways to do this. For me, my website offers a fantastic printing service ranging from wood, metal, canvas, glass, paper and more. There are a ton of sites and options for this for artists.

- Licensing: License your artwork for use on products like clothing, home decor, and stationery. Licensing agreements can provide a steady stream of passive income. Also, check out local hotels near you. Many of them would love to purchase a local artists prints to will their hallways with. Just ask. If you don't ask, the answer will always be no.
- Teaching and Workshops: Share your skills and knowledge by teaching art classes or workshops. This can be done in-person or online through platforms like Skillshare or Udemy. Many people would love for you to go to their home for a private lesson.
- Art Fairs and Markets: Participate in local art fairs and markets to sell your work directly to customers. These events can also be great for networking and gaining exposure. This is a great way to not only network, but also to fine tune your work. Seeing all of the artists and the way they set up and design their booths and sell their art is an invaluable way to level up your own game.

Adapting to Market Changes

The art market can be unpredictable, so it's important to stay adaptable and open to change. Here are some strategies to help you stay flexible:

- Stay Informed: Keep up with trends and changes in the art world. Subscribe to art magazines, follow industry blogs, and join professional organizations.
- Be Open to Feedback: Listen to feedback from clients, peers, and mentors. Use constructive criticism to improve your work and business practices.
- Experiment and Innovate: Don't be afraid to try new techniques, styles, or business models. Innovation can

set you apart and open up new opportunities. Always be learning something new.

Personal Growth and Continuous Learning

As an artist and business owner, continuous learning and personal growth are essential. Here's how to keep growing:

- Invest in Education: Take courses, attend workshops, and seek mentorship to continually improve your skills and knowledge.
- Read and Research: Read books on art, business, marketing, and personal development. Knowledge is a powerful tool for growth.
- Reflect and Adapt: Regularly reflect on your progress and adapt your strategies as needed. Set aside time to review your goals and achievements.

Conclusion of Chapter 3

Developing a business mindset is essential for turning your passion for art into a viable business. By understanding basic business principles, creating a solid business plan, building a strong brand, leveraging social media, networking, staying organized, exploring additional revenue streams, and continuously learning, you can set yourself up for success. In the next chapter, we'll explore how to build and expand your client base, an essential aspect of sustaining your art business.

Chapter 4: Building Your Client Base

Finding and Expanding Your Audience

Building a client base is essential for any successful art business. Your clients are the foundation of your income and can provide valuable feedback and opportunities for growth. When I first started my art business, identifying and reaching my ideal audience was a crucial step. And you'll find that many will become lifelong repeat customers of your work.

Identifying Your Target Market

When I began, I knew I wanted to focus on creating custom portraits. My ideal clients were individuals and families looking for unique, personalized art pieces. To refine my target market, I considered factors like age, income level, interests, and location. This helped me focus not only my art products, but also my marketing efforts more effectively.

Researching Your Market

Understanding where your target clients spend their time and money is vital. I researched the types of events they attended, the social media platforms they used, and the kinds of art they purchased. This research guided my marketing strategies and helped me connect with potential clients more effectively.

Reaching Out to Potential Clients

Once I identified my target audience, the next step was to reach out to them. Here are some strategies I used:

Social Media Marketing

Social media became a powerful tool for me. I used platforms like Instagram and Facebook to showcase my work and engage with my audience. By posting regularly, using relevant hashtags, and interacting with my followers, I was able to build a strong online presence. One of my early successes came from a post that went viral, bringing in a flood of inquiries and commissions.

Email Marketing

Building an email list was another effective strategy. I collected emails at art shows and through my website, then sent regular newsletters with updates on my work, upcoming events, and special offers. Tools like Mailchimp made managing my email campaigns easy and efficient. Learn to use this and integrate this in to your website and social media platforms. This will be a game changer for your email marketing.

Networking Events

Attending local art shows, exhibitions, and industry events provided great opportunities to meet potential clients and build relationships. I always carried business cards and was ready to talk about my work. One memorable connection was made at a local gallery opening, which led to a lucrative commission project. Also, each of my painting parties were basically mini networking events, and I would leave every party with new clients wanting new commissions or bookings. Networking was crucial to my business success.

Online Marketplaces

Listing my work on online art platforms like Etsy, Pinterest, facebook and Instagram helped me reach a wider audience. These sites have built-in audiences and can be a great way to showcase your work to potential buyers worldwide. And all of them have ways of advertising to any sort of segments of the population you wish. Very useful.

Building Relationships with Clients

Building strong relationships with clients can lead to repeat business and referrals. Here's how I fostered lasting connections:

Providing Excellent Customer Service

I made it a priority to respond promptly to inquiries, be courteous, and go the extra mile to ensure client satisfaction. A positive experience often turned one-time buyers into loyal clients who came back for more.

Following Up

After each sale, I followed up with a thank-you email or note, asking for feedback and letting clients know I was available for future projects. This simple gesture often led to additional commissions and referrals.

Offering Exclusive Deals

Rewarding loyal clients with special offers, discounts, or early access to new work helped encourage repeat purchases and referrals. For example, I usually offer a special discount to clients who had previously purchased my work, which resulted in several new commissions.

Personalizing Communication

Tailoring my communication to each client's preferences was key. I used their names, remembered past purchases, and showed genuine interest in their needs and feedback. This personal touch made clients feel valued and appreciated.

Leveraging Referrals and Word-of-Mouth

Word-of-mouth and referrals are powerful tools for building your client base. Here's how I encouraged them:

Asking for Referrals

I wasn't afraid to ask satisfied clients to refer me to their friends and family. Offering a referral discount or incentive as a thank you often prompted them to spread the word about my work.

Creating Shareable Content

Making it easy for clients to share my work by creating high-quality images, videos, and social media posts was crucial. Encouraging them to tag me in their posts and share their purchases helped increase my visibility. I would always have my portrait commissions pose for a photo holding their portraits. Even the dogs would pose for their pet portraits. The clients loved this and were excited to share with all of their friends and family on social media.

Hosting Referral Contests

Running referral contests where clients could win a prize for referring the most new customers created buzz and brought in new business. One successful contest I ran offered a free custom portrait to the client who referred the most new customers in a month.

Collaborating with Other Businesses

Partnering with businesses that complemented my work, such as interior designers, event planners, or photographers, led to valuable referrals. For instance, collaborating with a local photographer friend allowed us to cross-promote our services, which expanded our client base. And collaborating with different wine bars was a great way to meet many new locals eager to spend money on my art. Many even became lifelong clients and friends.

Utilizing Online and Offline Marketing Strategies

A balanced marketing approach that includes both online and offline strategies can help you reach a broader audience. Here are some tactics I used:

Online Marketing

SEO (Search Engine Optimization)

Optimizing my website for search engines increased organic traffic. I used relevant keywords, created valuable content, and ensured my site was mobile-friendly. This helped potential clients find me more easily. This was very time consuming and I had to research in order to learn how to do it, but it really made a difference. Also making sure you're listed on all search engines such as google so clients can look you up.

Content Marketing

Creating a blog to share my expertise and attract potential clients was another effective strategy. I wrote about art techniques, behind-the-scenes looks at my process, and tips for displaying art. This content drove traffic to my website and established me as an authority in my field.

Paid Advertising

Investing in online ads on platforms like Google Ads, Facebook, and Instagram helped me reach a targeted audience. Testing different ad formats and tracking their performance allowed me to optimize my campaigns for better results. I got really good at facebook and Instagram adds where I was able to get a ton of traffic without hardly spending anything except minimal amounts. Playing around with different ways to utilize these features will make or break success and cost. So experiment until you find a good fit.

Offline Marketing

Print Materials

Distributing business cards, flyers, and brochures at local businesses, art fairs, and community centers was a great way to reach potential clients. Ensuring they included my contact information and a link to my website made it easy for interested parties to follow up. Use QR codes, and always be ready to hand out a good looking business card.

Networking Events

Attending local business networking events, art fairs, and gallery openings provided opportunities to meet potential clients and collaborators. Building these connections often led to new business opportunities, and also helped to sharpen my own art. I often learned something new in the way another artist was creating or displaying their work. This is very important for inspiration and guidance.

Workshops and Classes

Hosting workshops or classes in my community showcased my skills and attracted potential clients. This also positioned me as an expert in my field, further enhancing my reputation. Many clients wanted to have private lessons at their homes as well. Being able to teach something is a great way to learn more about the very thing you're teaching. Don't be shy. Be confident in your art and share. The client saw something that prompted them to ask you to teach them, so lean in to this and enjoy the mutual benefits of teaching your craft to someone else.

Creating an Engaging Online Presence

Your online presence is often the first impression potential clients have of your business. Here's how to make it engaging and professional:

Website

Creating a professional website that showcased my portfolio, provided information about my services, and included an easy way for clients to contact me was essential. Using high-quality images and ensuring the site was easy to navigate made a significant difference. You will spend a lot of time on this, and that's okay. It's an intimate extension of you and your art. This is worth the time, effort and money. For instance, my site I actually paid a monthly subscription for because it was also connected to a printing service so I could offer prints my art on not only canvas, but, paper, glass, metal, wood, and much more. This was essential in helping me to diversify.

Social Media Profiles

Maintaining active and engaging social media profiles on platforms where my target audience was most active helped build my brand. Posting regularly, sharing behind-the-scenes content, and interacting with followers created a loyal online community. This is something you will want to dedicate time to everyday. I made it a rule to try my best to respond to any messages or comments right away. Strike while the irons hot. And always be ready with links to share with a way for them to purchase something. People are impatient sometimes and might lose interest if you make them wait for you to figure it all out. Be ready and act quickly when the time comes.

Blog or Vlog

Starting a blog or vlog to share my knowledge and connect with my audience was another effective strategy. Regularly posting valuable content drove traffic to my website and established me as an authority in my field. I would also often post live facebook videos of me in my studio, sometimes just setting up and others actually working on a painting. Either way they love to see behind the scenes as well as the artist in action doing what they do best and love.

Email List

Building an email list and sending regular newsletters with updates on my work, upcoming events, and special offers kept me top-of-mind with potential and existing clients. This was an effective way to maintain ongoing relationships and encourage repeat business. Get in the habit of sending monthly newsletters if not more. Clients would love to subscribe and stay in-the-know of what's happening with you.

Measuring and Analyzing Your Efforts

To ensure your marketing efforts are effective, it's important to measure and analyze their impact. Here are some ways I tracked my progress:

Analytics Tools

Using tools like Google Analytics, social media insights, and email marketing analytics helped me track performance. Monitoring metrics like website traffic, social media engagement, and email open rates provided valuable insights. This was a huge game changer. I was able to see exactly who was interacting with my content, complete with detailed information on their data such as age, sex, location, and what platforms they were using, time of day, etc. This really helped me to adjust the content and timing of my ads for greater impact and effect.

Client Feedback

Regularly asking for feedback from clients helped me understand what was working and what needed improvement. Using this information to refine my strategies ensured I was meeting their needs. I would even follow up with clients a little time after purchasing to ask about their satisfaction and get insight in to their experience in hopes to see if there was anything I could do better for them next time. They really appreciated this and only further solidified them as long term, loyal clients.

Sales Data

Analyzing sales data to identify trends and patterns helped me understand which products or services were most popular and where to focus my efforts. This is major asset to have. The more data at your fingertips, the more options you give yourself. Good data can lead to towards a client that has been browsing your art and website for days even weeks, allowing you to reach out. For instance, my website has this built in, where I can actually see the info of who has been checking out my site, which products their looking at, and even if they have left an item in their shopping cart, which is a tremendous feature. Sometimes a simple reach out from us offering a 10% discount my be the tipping point where they pull the trigger and purchase your art. Google Analytics is a fantastic option as well.

Adjusting Your Strategy

Based on my analysis, I adjusted my marketing strategy as needed. Experimenting with different tactics and tracking their performance allowed me to continually improve my results.

Conclusion of Chapter 4

Building and expanding your client base is a continuous process that requires strategic planning, effective marketing, and strong relationships. By identifying your target market, reaching out to potential clients, providing excellent customer service, leveraging referrals, and utilizing both online and offline marketing strategies, you can create a sustainable and growing client base for your art business. In the next chapter, we'll explore the importance of forming strategic partnerships and how they can contribute to your success.

Chapter 5: Forming Strategic Partnerships

The Power of Collaboration

Strategic partnerships can significantly amplify your reach and resources, making it easier to grow your art business. Collaborating with others allows you to leverage each other's strengths and networks. When I was starting out, forming a strategic partnership with a friend who was a photographer was a game-changer for me. Here's how I approached and benefited from this collaboration.

Finding the Right Partner

When looking for a partner, it's essential to find someone whose skills and network complement your own. My photographer friend and I had a great relationship and a shared vision for what we wanted to achieve. Her photography business was well-established, and she had access to a client base that could benefit from my custom portrait services. This synergy made our partnership natural and beneficial for both of us.

Approaching Potential Partners

Approaching potential partners requires a clear proposal of what you can offer and how the partnership will be mutually beneficial. When I pitched the idea to my photographer friend, I focused on how our combined services could offer unique value to her clients and expand our reach. We brainstormed ways to integrate our offerings, such as providing custom portraits as part of her photography packages.

Setting Up the Partnership

We decided to create an LLC together, named "Creative Synergy LLC." This structure allowed us to offer various art-related services under one umbrella. Setting up the LLC involved legal and financial considerations, but it provided a solid foundation for our business. We each had clear roles and responsibilities, which helped avoid conflicts and ensured smooth operations.

Expanding Through Collaboration

Our partnership opened new doors. We managed to get involved with several high schools, offering "life portraits" for graduating seniors. These portraits captured their passions and aspirations, making them popular among students and parents alike. This collaboration significantly increased our client base and visibility.

Benefits of Strategic Partnerships

Strategic partnerships can provide numerous benefits, including:

- **Increased Reach**: Partnering with someone who has access to a different audience can expand your reach. For us, collaborating with a photographer introduced my work to her clients, many of whom became repeat customers.
- **Shared Resources**: Pooling resources can reduce costs and increase efficiency. We shared marketing

expenses and combined our creative skills to offer more comprehensive services.

• Enhanced Credibility: A partnership can enhance your credibility. Being associated with a reputable photographer boosted my reputation and helped attract more clients.

• Mutual Support: Having a partner provides emotional and professional support. We could bounce ideas off each other, share successes, and navigate challenges together.

Overcoming Challenges in Partnerships

While partnerships offer many benefits, they can also present challenges. Here's how we navigated some common issues:

Communication

Open and honest communication is vital. We scheduled regular meetings to discuss our progress, address any concerns, and plan future projects. This transparency helped prevent misunderstandings and kept us aligned.

Conflict Resolution

Conflicts are inevitable, but how you handle them matters. We agreed to address issues directly and constructively. When disagreements arose, we focused on finding solutions rather than placing blame. This approach maintained our working relationship and kept the business moving forward.

Maintaining Independence

While we collaborated closely, we also maintained our independent businesses. This arrangement allowed us to benefit from the partnership without losing our individual identities. For example, she continued her photography business, and I pursued personal art projects alongside our joint ventures.

Real-Life Examples of Successful Partnerships

Our partnership led to several successful projects that significantly impacted my career. Here are a few examples:

High School Senior Portraits

The "life portraits" for high school seniors were a major success. We partnered with local schools to offer these custom portraits as part of their senior year packages. This project not only brought in steady income but also increased our visibility in the community.

Painting Parties

Hosting painting parties was another successful venture. I collaborated with local wine bars and offered themed painting sessions. These events were hugely popular and became a significant source of income. Partnering with venues provided the space and clientele, while I provided the artistic expertise.

Pet Portraits

A chance meeting with a pet boutique owner led to another fruitful collaboration. We organized pet portrait painting parties, where pet owners could paint portraits of their pets. This niche market was incredibly lucrative, and the boutique's clientele provided a steady stream of customers.

How to Form Your Own Strategic Partnerships

Here are some steps to help you form your own strategic partnerships:

1. Identify Potential Partners: Look for businesses or individuals whose services complement yours. This could be photographers, event planners, interior designers, or local businesses.
2. Make a Clear Proposal: Outline how the partnership will be mutually beneficial. Highlight what you can offer and how it aligns with their goals.
3. Establish Clear Roles and Responsibilities: Define each partner's roles to avoid conflicts and ensure smooth operations.
4. Communicate Regularly: Maintain open and honest communication to address any issues promptly and keep the partnership on track.
5. Focus on Mutual Success: Approach the partnership with a mindset of mutual success. Celebrate each other's achievements and support each other through challenges.

Conclusion of Chapter 5

Forming strategic partnerships can significantly enhance your art business by expanding your reach, sharing resources, and providing mutual support. By finding the right partners, setting clear expectations, and maintaining open communication, you can create successful collaborations that drive growth and innovation. In the next chapter, we'll explore effective marketing strategies to help you expand your reach and attract more clients.

Chapter 6: Marketing and Expanding Your Reach

The Importance of Effective Marketing

Effective marketing is crucial for expanding your reach and attracting more clients. When I first started my art business, I quickly realized that creating beautiful art was only part of the equation. I needed to get my work in front of the right people. Here's how I developed and executed my marketing strategies to grow my business.

Understanding Your Audience

Understanding your audience is the foundation of any successful marketing strategy. I spent time researching my target market to learn about their preferences, spending habits, and where they spent their time online. This information was invaluable for tailoring my marketing efforts.

Building a Strong Online Presence

A strong online presence is essential for modern artists. Here's how I built mine:

Creating a Professional Website

I invested in a professional website that showcased my portfolio, provided information about my services, and made it easy for clients to contact me. High-quality images of my work and a clean, user-friendly design helped make a great first impression. I not only invested money, but my greatest investment in to this was my time. I did not have a lot of money starting out, so my goal was to do everything I could on my own. The downside to this was I had to teach myself how to set up a website, and also every step in between was on me. I had to learn how to take high quality images of all of my work, how to write SEO content for each product on my site, as well as all verbiage on my site as well. This took so much time. But in the end, I felt so proud of my hard work. My website ended up being an extension of me and felt like a child of mine.

Leveraging Social Media

Social media platforms like Instagram, Facebook, Etsy and Pinterest played a significant role in my marketing strategy. I posted regularly, shared behind-the-scenes content, and interacted with my followers. Here's what worked for me:

- Consistency: Posting regularly kept my audience engaged and increased my visibility.
- Engagement: Responding to comments, participating in discussions, and showing appreciation for my followers helped build a loyal community.
- Hashtags: Using relevant hashtags helped my posts reach a broader audience. I researched popular hashtags in the art community and experimented to see which ones worked best for my content.

Utilizing Content Marketing

Creating valuable content helped establish me as an authority in my field and attracted potential clients. I started a blog where I shared art techniques, behind-the-scenes looks at my process, and tips for displaying art. This content drove traffic to my website and provided value to my audience.

Email Marketing

Building an email list was another highly effective strategy. I collected emails at art shows, through my website, and from social media. Sending regular newsletters with updates, special offers, and insights kept my audience engaged and informed.

Offline Marketing Strategies

While online marketing is crucial, offline strategies also played a significant role in my success:

Networking Events

Attending local art shows, exhibitions, and industry events helped me meet potential clients and build relationships. One memorable connection was made at a local gallery opening, which led to a lucrative commission project.

Print Materials

I created high-quality business cards, flyers, and brochures to distribute at events and local businesses. These materials included my contact information and a link to my website, making it easy for interested parties to follow up.

Workshops and Classes

Hosting workshops and classes in my community showcased my skills and attracted potential clients. This also positioned me as an expert in my field and provided additional income streams.

Innovative Marketing Techniques

Thinking outside the box and trying new marketing techniques helped me stand out in a crowded market:

Painting Parties

One of the most successful marketing strategies I implemented was hosting painting parties. I collaborated with local wine bars to offer themed painting sessions. These events were hugely popular and became a significant source of income. Partnering with venues provided the space and clientele, while I provided the artistic expertise.

Pet Portraits

A chance meeting with a pet boutique owner led to another innovative marketing strategy. We organized pet portrait painting parties, where pet owners could paint portraits of their pets. This niche market was incredibly lucrative, and the boutique's clientele provided a steady stream of customers.

Live Painting Events

I also started offering live painting at events, such as weddings and corporate functions. This not only provided a unique service but also showcased my skills to a broader audience. The guests at these events often became new clients, commissioning custom pieces or attending my workshops.

Measuring and Analyzing Your Efforts

To ensure my marketing efforts were effective, I regularly measured and analyzed their impact:

Analytics Tools

Using tools like Google Analytics, social media insights, and email marketing analytics helped me track performance. Monitoring metrics like website traffic, social media engagement, and email open rates provided valuable insights.

Client Feedback

Regularly asking for feedback from clients helped me understand what was working and what needed improvement. Using this information to refine my strategies ensured I was meeting their needs.

Sales Data

Analyzing sales data to identify trends and patterns helped me understand which products or services were most popular and where to focus my efforts.

Adjusting Your Strategy

Based on my analysis, I adjusted my marketing strategy as needed. Experimenting with different tactics and tracking their performance allowed me to continually improve my results.

Real-Life Examples of Marketing Success

Here are some real-life examples of how my marketing efforts paid off:

Social Media Success

One of my Instagram posts showcasing a recent commission went viral, bringing in a flood of inquiries and new followers. The engagement from that single post resulted in several new commissions and increased visibility for my work.

Email Campaigns

An email campaign announcing a new series of prints resulted in a significant spike in sales. By offering a limited-time discount to my email subscribers, I created a sense of urgency that encouraged quick purchases.

Local Collaborations

Collaborating with local businesses, such as wine bars and pet boutiques, provided mutually beneficial marketing opportunities. These partnerships not only brought in new clients but also enhanced my reputation in the community.

Conclusion of Chapter 6

Effective marketing is essential for expanding your reach and attracting more clients. By understanding your audience, building a strong online presence, leveraging content marketing, utilizing email marketing, implementing offline strategies, and measuring your efforts, you can create a comprehensive marketing plan that drives growth. In the next chapter, we'll explore innovative business models that can help you diversify your income and adapt to market changes.

Chapter 7: Innovative Business Models

Diversifying Your Income

Diversifying your income is crucial for stability and growth in an art business. Relying solely on one source of income can be risky, especially in the unpredictable art market. Here's how I diversified my income streams and developed innovative business models to sustain my art career.

Exploring Multiple Revenue Streams

Early in my career, I realized the importance of having multiple income streams. This not only provided financial stability but also allowed me to explore different aspects of my creativity. Here are some ways I diversified my income:

Commissions and Custom Art

One of the first revenue streams I focused on was commissions. Creating custom pieces for clients provided a steady income. I promoted this service through my website and social media, showcasing examples of past commissions, and of course by in person and word of mouth. Custom portraits, in particular, became a significant part of my business. By offering personalized art, I could cater to clients' specific needs and tastes.

Prints and Reproductions

Offering prints of my work allowed me to reach a broader audience. I researched high-quality printing services and created a range of print options, from affordable paper prints to premium canvas reproductions. Selling prints online through my website and platforms like Etsy helped increase my reach and sales.

Licensing Agreements

Licensing my artwork for use on products like clothing, home decor, and stationery provided a steady stream of passive income. I reached out to companies that aligned with my brand and negotiated licensing deals. This not only generated income but also increased exposure for my work.

Teaching and Workshops

Teaching art classes and workshops became another valuable revenue stream. I started by offering local workshops, then expanded to online classes. Platforms like Skillshare and Udemy provided a global audience for my courses. Teaching allowed me to share my knowledge and passion while earning income.

Live Painting Events

Offering live painting at events, such as weddings and corporate functions, became a unique service that set me apart. These events not only provided income but also showcased my skills to a broader audience. The guests at these events often became new clients, commissioning custom pieces or attending my workshops.

Developing Niche Markets

Finding and developing niche markets helped me stand out in a crowded market. Here's how I identified and capitalized on niche opportunities:

Pet Portraits

A chance meeting with a pet boutique owner led to the idea of offering pet portraits. This niche market was incredibly lucrative. We organized pet portrait painting parties, where pet owners could paint portraits of their pets. The boutique's clientele provided a steady stream of customers, and word-of-mouth referrals kept the business growing and the sales easily trickled to not only the painting parties but also, many of the clients purchased high end oil portraits for their pets and their families as well.

Wine Glass Painting Parties

I noticed that painting parties were becoming popular, but I wanted to offer something unique. I came up with the idea of wine glass painting parties. Partnering with local wine bars, I hosted themed painting sessions where participants painted designs on wine glasses. These events were hugely popular and became a significant source of income.

Adapting to Market Changes

The art market can be unpredictable, so it's important to stay adaptable and open to change. Here are some strategies that helped me stay flexible:

Staying Informed

I kept up with trends and changes in the art world by subscribing to art magazines, following industry blogs, and joining professional organizations. This helped me stay ahead of the curve and adapt my business strategies accordingly.

Listening to Feedback

I regularly asked for feedback from clients, peers, and mentors. Using constructive criticism to improve my work and business practices was crucial. This feedback helped me refine my services and better meet my clients' needs.

Experimenting and Innovating

I wasn't afraid to try new techniques, styles, or business models. Innovation set me apart and opened up new opportunities. For example, when I noticed the growing interest in eco-friendly products, I started offering artwork on recycled materials and promoting sustainable practices in my business.

Personal Growth and Continuous Learning

As an artist and business owner, continuous learning and personal growth are essential. Here's how I kept growing:

Investing in Education

I took courses, attended workshops, and sought mentorship to continually improve my skills and knowledge. Investing in my education paid off by keeping my work fresh and relevant. I often spent countless hours in my free time learning a new skill, such as animation and digital art for logos, etc.

Reading and Researching

I read books on art, business, marketing, and personal development. Knowledge is a powerful tool for growth, and staying informed helped me make better business decisions.

Reflecting and Adapting

I regularly reflected on my progress and adapted my strategies as needed. Setting aside time to review my goals and achievements helped me stay focused and motivated.

Real-Life Examples of Innovative Business Models

Here are some real-life examples of how innovative business models contributed to my success:

Collaborative Projects

Collaborating with other artists and businesses opened up new opportunities. For example, I partnered with a local coffee shop to display my artwork. We also held monthly painting parties there. This increased their business as well as mine. The coffee shop's clientele became my potential clients, and we both benefited from the increased exposure.

Seasonal Promotions

Running seasonal promotions and themed art series helped boost sales. For instance, I created a series of holiday-themed prints that became popular gifts. Promoting these series through email campaigns and social media generated significant sales during peak seasons.

Pop-Up Galleries

Setting up pop-up galleries in non-traditional spaces, like local boutiques and community centers, allowed me to reach new audiences. These temporary exhibits created buzz and drew in visitors who might not visit a traditional gallery.

Conclusion of Chapter 7

Diversifying your income and developing innovative business models are essential for sustaining and growing your art business. By exploring multiple revenue streams, adapting to market changes, and continually investing in your personal growth, you can create a resilient and thriving art business. In the next chapter, we'll discuss how to handle setbacks and failures, turning them into opportunities for growth and success.

Chapter 8: Handling Setbacks and Failures

Embracing Failure as a Catalyst for Success

Setbacks and failures are inevitable in any business, and the art world is no exception. My journey was filled with challenges that often seemed insurmountable, but each failure taught me valuable lessons and ultimately fueled my success. Here's how I learned to embrace failure and turn setbacks into opportunities.

The Early Setback: Ringling College

One of my earliest and most significant setbacks was not being able to attend Ringling College of Art and Design. Despite being accepted and offered a full scholarship, the additional costs and the program's intensity made it financially impossible for me to attend. This nearly broke me, but it also ignited a determination to find an alternative path to success.

Learning from Failure

Each failure provided an opportunity to learn and grow. When I couldn't attend Ringling, I had to find other ways to improve my skills and build my career. I took online courses, attended workshops, and sought mentorship from established artists. This self-directed learning not only honed my skills but also taught me resilience and resourcefulness.

The Partnership That Fell Apart

Forming a partnership with my photographer friend was initially a great success. We created "Creative Synergy LLC" and moved our business to Texas, believing the booming economy would support our growth. However, our partnership faced challenges, and personal conflicts led to its dissolution. This was a significant setback, but it also became a catalyst for my ultimate success.

Picking Up the Pieces

After the partnership fell apart, I found myself in a new state, away from family, and temporarily living with my cousin. I felt defeated, but I refused to give up. I got a job as a server to make ends meet and dedicated all my free time to rebuilding my art business. This period of hard work and sacrifice taught me the value of perseverance and adaptability.

Turning Failure into Opportunity

Failure often opens new doors and provides unexpected opportunities. For example, the end of my partnership forced me to rethink my business model and find new ways to market my work. This led to the development of successful initiatives like painting parties and pet portraits, which became significant revenue streams.

Strategies for Overcoming Setbacks

Here are some strategies that helped me overcome setbacks and turn failures into opportunities:

Stay Resilient

Resilience is crucial when facing setbacks. It's important to stay focused on your goals and not let failures deter you. Each challenge is an opportunity to learn and grow. For example, when my partnership ended, I didn't see it as the end of my dreams but as a chance to rebuild stronger. Building blocks, or stepping stones; its all in how you use them.

Adapt and Pivot

Be willing to adapt and pivot your strategies when things don't go as planned. After the partnership dissolved, I had to find new ways to reach clients and generate income. This led me to explore innovative business models and diversify my income streams.

Seek Support

Don't be afraid to seek support from friends, family, and mentors. Their encouragement and advice can provide valuable perspective and help you stay motivated. During my tough times, having a supportive network was crucial in keeping me focused and positive.

Reflect and Learn

Take time to reflect on your failures and understand what went wrong. Use these insights to make better decisions in the future. Each setback is a learning experience that can guide you toward success.

Stay Positive

Maintaining a positive mindset is essential. Focus on your achievements and the progress you've made, rather than dwelling on failures. This positive outlook will help you stay motivated and resilient in the face of challenges.

Personal Examples of Turning Setbacks into Success

The Wine Glass Painting Parties

After moving to Texas and facing the end of my partnership, I needed a new way to generate income and reach clients. I came up with the idea of wine glass painting parties. Partnering with local wine bars, I hosted themed painting sessions where participants painted designs on wine glasses. These events were hugely popular and became a significant source of income, demonstrating how a creative idea can turn a setback into a success.

Pet Portraits

Another example is the development of my pet portrait business. After meeting a pet boutique owner, I saw an opportunity to offer pet portrait painting parties. This niche market was incredibly lucrative and provided a steady stream of customers. By adapting my services to meet market demands, I turned a chance encounter into a successful business venture.

Moving Forward After Failure

Moving forward after a failure requires a clear plan and determination. Here's how I did it:

Setting New Goals

After each setback, I set new goals to stay focused and motivated. These goals were specific, measurable, and achievable, providing a clear path forward. For example, after the end of my partnership, my goal was to rebuild my client base and develop new revenue streams.

Revisiting Your Business Plan

It's important to revisit and revise your business plan after a failure. This helps you realign your strategies and adapt to new circumstances. I updated my business plan to include new initiatives like painting parties and online sales, which helped me stay on track.

Continuous Improvement

Commit to continuous improvement in all aspects of your business. This includes honing your skills, staying informed about market trends, and seeking feedback from clients. Continuous improvement ensures that you are always moving forward and adapting to changes.

Conclusion of Chapter 8

Setbacks and failures are inevitable, but they can also be powerful catalysts for growth and success. By staying resilient, adapting to change, seeking support, and maintaining a positive mindset, you can turn failures into opportunities. In the next chapter, we'll explore how to scale your business and achieve long-term success.

Chapter 9: Scaling Your Business

Transitioning from Local to National (or Global) Reach

Scaling your art business involves expanding beyond your local market to reach a broader audience. This transition requires careful planning, strategic marketing, and sometimes, a bit of trial and error. Here's how I managed to scale my business and the lessons I learned along the way.

Starting Small and Thinking Big

Initially, my focus was on building a strong local presence. I participated in local art fairs, collaborated with nearby businesses, and hosted workshops and painting parties. Establishing a solid reputation locally provided a strong foundation for scaling up.

Building a Robust Online Presence

To reach a broader audience, I knew I had to establish a strong online presence. Here's what worked for me:

Professional Website

My website became the hub of my online presence. I invested in professional web design to ensure it was visually appealing and easy to navigate. High-quality images of my work, detailed descriptions, and an easy-to-use contact form made it easy for visitors to learn about my art and reach out.

E-commerce Integration

Adding an e-commerce section to my website allowed me to sell prints, original works, and custom commissions directly to customers. This not only increased my sales but also made my art accessible to a global audience. This was also a great way to share my portfolio with others.

Social Media Marketing

Social media platforms like Instagram, Facebook, and Pinterest played a crucial role in scaling my business. Here's how I used them effectively:

- Consistency: Posting regularly kept my audience engaged and increased my visibility.
- Engagement: Responding to comments, participating in discussions, and showing appreciation for my followers helped build a loyal community.
- Hashtags: Using relevant hashtags helped my posts reach a broader audience. I researched popular hashtags in the art community and experimented to see which ones worked best for my content.

Photographing My Work

High-quality images are crucial for showcasing your art online. However, I couldn't afford to hire a professional photographer, so I set up a system to photograph my work using just my iPhone. Here's how I achieved visually appealing, high-quality images:

- Good Lighting: Natural light is your best friend. I took photos during the day near large windows to ensure my artwork was well-lit and colors were accurately represented. When natural light wasn't sufficient, I used affordable softbox lights to create an even, diffused light source. For my glasses, in the beginning, when I was on a budget
- Pleasing Backgrounds: I used neutral backgrounds that didn't distract from the artwork. A simple white or black backdrop worked well for most pieces. For larger works, I hung a clean white sheet behind the artwork.
- Stable Setup: To avoid blurry images, I used a tripod to keep my iPhone steady. This ensured that every shot was sharp and professional-looking.
- Editing: After taking the photos, I used editing apps like Snapseed and Lightroom to adjust brightness, contrast, and color balance, ensuring the images accurately represented the original artwork.

This DIY approach to photography saved costs and allowed me to produce high-quality images for my website, e-commerce platforms, and social media.

Email Marketing

Building an email list was another effective strategy. I collected emails at art shows, through my website, and from social media. Sending regular newsletters with updates, special offers, and insights kept my audience engaged and informed.

Expanding Through Collaborations

Collaborating with other artists and businesses helped expand my reach. Here are some successful collaborations:

Partnerships with Local Businesses

Partnering with local wine bars for painting parties and pet boutiques for pet portrait events provided mutual benefits. These partnerships not only brought in new clients but also enhanced my reputation in the community.

Online Collaborations

Collaborating with other online artists and influencers helped me reach a new audience. We co-hosted online workshops, shared each other's work on social media, and even created joint art pieces. These collaborations introduced my work to a broader audience and opened up new opportunities.

Exhibitions and Art Fairs

Participating in national and international art fairs and exhibitions was a game-changer. These events provided exposure to a larger audience and the opportunity to network with other artists, gallery owners, and potential clients. One of my most memorable experiences was exhibiting at a major art fair in Texas, where I made valuable connections and significantly increased my sales. This also, started a trend where I attended these shows yearly, adding an entirely new revenue stream for me and my artwork.

Leveraging Technology

Technology played a vital role in scaling my business. Here are some tools and platforms that made a difference:

Art Marketplaces

Listing my work on online art marketplaces like Saatchi Art, Etsy, and Artfinder helped me reach a global audience. These platforms have built-in audiences and can be a great way to showcase your work to potential buyers worldwide.

Digital Marketing Tools

Using digital marketing tools like Google Ads, Facebook Ads, and Instagram Ads allowed me to target specific demographics and increase my visibility. By testing different ad formats and tracking their performance, I optimized my campaigns for better results.

Project Management Tools

Tools like Trello, Hootsuite, Asana, and Monday helped me manage projects, deadlines, and tasks efficiently. Staying organized ensured that I could handle the increased workload that came with scaling my business.

Expanding Your Product Offerings

Diversifying your product offerings can attract a wider audience and increase your sales. Here's how I expanded my product line:

Prints and Merchandise

Offering prints and merchandise like t-shirts, mugs, and phone cases allowed me to reach customers who might not be able to afford original pieces. These products were popular gifts and provided a steady stream of income.

Workshops and Online Courses

Expanding my workshops and offering online courses allowed me to share my knowledge with a global audience. My focus was, over time, turning towards residual income. I felt the best way to expand would be to slowly phase myself out of doing everything my self, and hopefully find a product or a process that could be manufactured, so to speak, so that my hands wouldn't have to be literally touching every single sale. Since I was running everything by myself, I either needed to hire help to train and eventually take over, or come up with a system or product that I could create once, and continually make money off of selling. I had to start thinking about retirement.

Custom Commissions

Offering custom commissions for portraits, pet portraits, and other personalized art pieces became a significant part of my business. Promoting this service through my website and social media attracted clients looking for unique, personalized art. But, my biggest way to promote these was word of mouth, and in person at my events.

Managing Growth and Maintaining Quality

As my business grew, it was essential to maintain the quality of my work and customer service. Here's how I managed growth:

Outsourcing and Delegating

To handle the increased workload, I began outsourcing tasks like website maintenance, marketing, and accounting. This allowed me to focus on creating art while ensuring that other aspects of my business ran smoothly.

Hiring Assistants

Hiring assistants helped manage day-to-day operations and larger projects. For example, during busy periods, having an assistant to help with packaging and shipping orders was invaluable. This is a great way to offer part-time jobs to your local community. Not only was I able to hire on my cousin's teenage daughter, but, I also got involved in the local university and was blessed to offer college credit for college students needed service hours. This was an amazing experience and I was able to have great help and without having to pay.

Continuous Improvement

I committed to continuous improvement in all aspects of my business. This included honing my skills, staying informed about market trends, and seeking feedback from clients. Continuous improvement ensured that I could meet the growing demands of my business while maintaining high standards.

Personal Story: Overcoming the Challenges of Scaling

Scaling my business wasn't without its challenges. Here are some personal experiences that shaped my journey:

Managing Work-Life Balance

As my business grew, managing work-life balance became increasingly difficult. I often found myself working late into the night and sacrificing personal time. Recognizing the importance of balance, I started setting boundaries, scheduling regular breaks, and prioritizing self-care. This not only improved my well-being but also made me more productive and creative.

Handling Increased Demand

With increased demand came the pressure to deliver high-quality work consistently. I learned to manage this by setting realistic deadlines, communicating clearly with clients, and not being afraid to say no when necessary. Understanding my limits and managing client expectations were crucial for maintaining quality and avoiding burnout.

Navigating Financial Challenges

Scaling my business required significant financial investment, from marketing and website development to attending art fairs and exhibitions. I managed these challenges by creating a detailed budget, seeking financial advice, and reinvesting profits back into my business. This careful financial planning ensured that I could sustain growth without compromising my financial stability.

Conclusion of Chapter 9

Scaling your art business involves expanding your reach, leveraging technology, diversifying your product offerings, and managing growth effectively. By building a robust online presence, collaborating with others, utilizing digital tools, maintaining high-quality images, and managing your workload efficiently, you can achieve long-term success. In the next chapter, we'll explore how to sustain your success and continue evolving your business over time.

Chapter 10: Achieving Long-term Success

Sustaining Your Success

Achieving initial success in your art business is an incredible milestone, but sustaining that success over the long term requires continuous effort, innovation, and strategic planning. Here's how I managed to maintain and grow my business over the years, along with the lessons I learned and the strategies I employed.

Continuous Improvement and Learning

Staying relevant in the art world means continuously improving your skills and staying informed about industry trends. Here's how I committed to lifelong learning:

Investing in Education

I took courses, attended workshops, and sought mentorship to continually improve my skills and knowledge. This commitment to education kept my work fresh and relevant, allowing me to adapt to new trends and techniques. For example, I enrolled in online classes to learn advanced digital art techniques, which opened up new avenues for commissions and collaborations. I was constantly playing with new technology and techniques. I would see what others were doing on social media and want to emulate this. I would get me the latest IPad for my business, but instead of just using it for business alone, I would spend countless hours teaching myself how to use the latest app for creating high quality art, such as Procreate. Procreate was a game changer for me. Previously I had to teach myself how to use photoshop, which is very expensive, and hard to use. But with procreate, they managed to bring high end photo editing abilities, previously only found on high end apps like photoshop, but for a fraction of the cost. And, it was a ton of fun to use apple's stylus.

Reading and Researching

I read books on art, business, marketing, and personal development. Knowledge is a powerful tool for growth, and staying informed helped me make better business decisions. For instance, reading about social media algorithms and SEO techniques enabled me to optimize my online presence and reach a wider audience. I was constantly adapting and updating my sites and you should be doing this too. Stay fresh. This is not only important for your own benefit and your own craft, but, the busier you look to your clients, the more successful you look. And the more successful you look, the more they want to buy art from you. It's as simple as that.

Reflecting and Adapting

I regularly reflected on my progress and adapted my strategies as needed. Setting aside time to review my goals and achievements helped me stay focused and motivated. I kept a journal where I documented my successes and challenges, which provided valuable insights into what worked and what didn't. I even kept a "to-do-list" in my notes app on my phone. I did this so I could easily write down an idea I had while out and about if I saw something that I noticed another business was doing, so that I could investigate and potentially implement the same thing for my business if it turned out to be beneficial or feasible.

Building Strong Client Relationships

Maintaining strong relationships with clients is key to long-term success. Here's how I fostered lasting connections:

Providing Excellent Customer Service

I made it a priority to respond promptly to inquiries, be courteous, and go the extra mile to ensure client satisfaction. A positive experience often turned one-time buyers into loyal clients who came back for more. One memorable instance was when a client needed a last-minute commission for a special occasion. I worked overtime to meet the deadline, and the client was so impressed that they referred several friends to my business. I always tried to say yes when possible.

Following Up

After each sale, I followed up with a thank-you email or note, asking for feedback and letting clients know I was available for future projects. This simple gesture often led to additional commissions and referrals. For example, a thank-you note to a client who purchased a pet portrait led to multiple referrals within their pet owner community.

Offering Exclusive Deals

Rewarding loyal clients with special offers, discounts, or early access to new work helped encourage repeat purchases and referrals. For example, I once offered a special discount to clients who had previously purchased my work, which resulted in several new commissions.

Personalizing Communication

Tailoring my communication to each client's preferences was key. I used their names, remembered past purchases, and showed genuine interest in their needs and feedback. This personal touch made clients feel valued and appreciated. For instance, sending personalized holiday greetings to clients helped strengthen our relationships and kept me top-of-mind for future projects.

Expanding Your Network

Networking is crucial for long-term success. Building relationships with other artists, galleries, and industry professionals can open up new opportunities. Here's how I expanded my network:

Attending Events

I regularly attended art shows, exhibitions, and industry events. These were great opportunities to meet other artists, gallery owners, and potential clients. One significant connection was made at an art fair where I met a gallery owner who later hosted a solo exhibition of my work, significantly boosting my visibility and sales. And, often at these events, I would run in to another owners that wanted to work with me at their business. Most of my sales and marketing success came from direct face to face communication and word of mouth advertising. I knew going in that this was the best form of advertising as well as the cheapest.

Joining Online Communities

Participating in online forums, social media groups, and artist networks provided support, feedback, and new opportunities. For example, joining a popular online art community led to several collaborative projects with other artists, expanding my reach and audience.

Following Up

After meeting someone, I followed up with a message or email to keep in touch and build genuine relationships. This practice not only helped maintain connections but also led to new business opportunities. For example, following up with a curator I met at an event resulted in an invitation to participate in a group exhibition.

Leveraging Technology for Efficiency

Technology played a crucial role in maintaining and growing my business. Here are some tools and platforms that helped me stay efficient:

Project Management Tools

Using project management tools like Trello, Asana, and Monday helped me manage projects, deadlines, and tasks efficiently. And also, simple tools, like my notes app in my iPhone. I started with this before switching to more expensive ones. Start with what you have available within your means, and gradually grow with you business. Apps like Workplace, Google ads, Mailchimp, Teamup and Eventbrite, were hugely beneficial. These tools allowed me to keep track of ongoing projects, communicate with clients, and ensure timely delivery of my work.

Financial Management Software

Software like QuickBooks, FreshBooks and Square helped me manage my finances, track expenses, and generate invoices. This made it easier to stay on top of my financial health and ensure timely payments. I particularly loved using Square, because it had a built in invoice generator that was essential for me to send clients an invoice for them to pay from using whatever form of payment they wished.

Digital Marketing Tools

Digital marketing tools like Google Analytics, social media insights, and email marketing platforms like MailChimp provided valuable data on my marketing efforts. This data helped me refine my strategies and optimize my campaigns for better results.

Staying Creative and Inspired

Maintaining creativity and finding inspiration is essential for an artist's long-term success. Here's how I stayed inspired:

Exploring New Mediums and Techniques

I regularly experimented with new mediums and techniques to keep my work fresh and exciting. This not only expanded my skill set but also attracted new clients interested in diverse styles. For example, learning to create digital art allowed me to offer digital commissions and broaden my portfolio. I put in the time to play with new technology and learn new techniques. This was fun, because, as an artist, I felt very comfortable on my own doodling or sketching. I would often grab my new iPad and stylus and sit outside with some coffee and just sketch some birds or flowers and try to get as good at using the app as the amazing artists I was seeing online, who had obviously been trained and spent a ridiculous amount of time with the app to be so comfortable.

Traveling and Experiencing New Cultures

Traveling and experiencing new cultures provided endless inspiration for my work. Visiting art museums, galleries, and cultural sites sparked new ideas and influenced my artistic style. A trip to Europe, where I explored the works of the Old Masters, inspired a new series of portraits that became very popular with my clients. Everywhere I went, I was checking out the way other business were run, as well as other artists and their work. It was amazing to see from the view of a business owner. This was essential in me getting out of my own head and really marketing myself and figuring out how to sell my work.

Collaborating with Other Artists

Collaborating with other artists introduced me to different perspectives and techniques. These collaborations often resulted in unique pieces that attracted attention and new clients. For instance, a collaboration with a sculptor led to a mixed-media series that garnered significant interest and sales.

Personal Story: Overcoming the Challenges of Sustaining Success

Sustaining success wasn't without its challenges. Here are some personal experiences that shaped my journey:

Managing Burnout

As my business grew, the risk of burnout increased. I often found myself overwhelmed by the demands of running a successful art business. Recognizing the signs of burnout, I made self-care a priority. I scheduled regular breaks, practiced mindfulness, and ensured I had time for hobbies and relaxation. This not only improved my well-being but also made me more productive and creative. I cannot stress this enough. You MUST make time for yourself to do the things you enjoy, otherwise you will lose all interest, because it is hard running a business. Keeping yourself balanced and relaxed, and able to still have fun with everything is where the magic happens.

Navigating Market Changes

The art market is constantly evolving, and staying relevant required adaptability. When traditional art fairs and galleries faced challenges, I pivoted to online sales and virtual exhibitions. This flexibility allowed me to reach new audiences and sustain my business through market fluctuations. Always be ready and willing to adjust. If we're paying attention, we can often see when these trends or transitions are on the horizon and already be investigating and ready to adjust by the time change comes. The only thing that is constant in life is change. So be ready at all times, to adjust your sails to better catch the wind.

Balancing Personal and Professional Life

Balancing personal and professional life was crucial for long-term success. I set clear boundaries between work and personal time, ensuring I could dedicate quality time to both. This balance not only improved my personal relationships but also allowed me to bring fresh energy and focus to my work. Without this I would have burned out before I even started. I spend countless hours just reading books and watching movies and going out with friends. The entire time, in the back of my mind, I always viewing everything through a lens of how this could work with my business; and how could I implement something like this.

Conclusion of Chapter 10

Achieving long-term success in your art business requires continuous improvement, building strong client relationships, expanding your network, leveraging technology, staying creative, and overcoming challenges. By committing to lifelong learning, maintaining high standards, and staying adaptable, you can sustain and grow your art business over time. In the next chapter, we'll explore the future of your art business and how to plan for continued growth and success.

Chapter 11: Planning for Continued Growth and Success

Vision for the Future

Planning for the future is crucial for the continued growth and success of your art business. Setting short-term goals is important; yes, but setting long-term goals, staying adaptable, and continuously innovating will ensure that your business remains relevant and thriving. Here's how I approached planning for the future and the steps I took to ensure sustained success.

Setting Long-term Goals

Setting clear, achievable long-term goals provided direction and motivation. Here's how I set and pursued these goals:

Defining Success

Success can mean different things to different people. For me, success was not only financial stability but also personal fulfillment and artistic growth. I took time to define what success meant to me, which helped shape my long-term goals. For example, one of my goals was to have my work exhibited in prestigious galleries, which required building a strong portfolio and networking with gallery owners. I wasn't attempting to get rich. I was interested in being able to pay all of my bills and live comfortably by doing something that I love. This helped me to stay focused.

I was more interested in slow, organic growth, rather than getting rich fast. This mindset is crucial, because good things rarely happen fast; good things take time. Patience and perseverance is key.

Creating a Vision Board

I created a vision board to visualize my goals and aspirations. This included images and quotes that inspired me, as well as specific milestones I wanted to achieve. Keeping this vision board in my studio served as a constant reminder of what I was working towards. I'm not kidding. I surrounded myself with all sorts of inspiration at all times. Whether they were screensavers on my computer or on my iPhone, I was constantly inundated with inspiration. I was constantly saving quotes and images that inspired me. When you have a plan to start something, work it out on paper first. Make sure you can actually see the beginning, middle and end of the process and all of the steps in between. This will help to implement and not get discouraged so easily.

Breaking Down Goals into Actionable Steps

Breaking down long-term goals into smaller, actionable steps made them more manageable. For instance, if my goal was to increase my online sales, I broke it down into tasks like improving my website, optimizing SEO, and running targeted ad campaigns. This step-by-step approach ensured steady progress towards my larger goals.

Adapting to Industry Trends

Staying ahead of industry trends is essential for maintaining relevance and competitiveness. Here's how I adapted to changes in the art market:

Keeping Up with Technology

The art market is increasingly digital, and staying updated with technology was crucial. I learned to use digital tools and platforms to reach a wider audience. For example, I explored virtual reality (VR) to create immersive art experiences and augmented reality (AR) to allow clients to visualize my work in their spaces. My website had an amazing feature where they could see what my artwork would look like on their walls. They could change the frame, the size, and literally see through their iPad or iPhone, or whatever device they were on, what my artwork looked like in any space in their home. This was an amazing feature and the customers loved using this. I loved using this as well, because art is very visual. Sometimes the only thing hindering a sale is the client not being able to visualize something for themselves.

Exploring New Art Forms

Exploring new art forms and mediums kept my work fresh and exciting. I experimented with digital art, installation art, and mixed media. These new forms not only expanded my skill set but also attracted a broader audience interested in contemporary art.

Participating in Online Communities

Joining online art communities and forums kept me informed about industry trends and innovations. These communities provided valuable insights, feedback, and networking opportunities. For example, participating in a popular online art forum led to a collaborative project with other artists, which was showcased in a virtual gallery.

Expanding Your Brand

Expanding your brand involves reaching new markets, diversifying your offerings, and maintaining a strong identity. Here's how I expanded my brand:

Rebranding for Growth

As my business grew, I rebranded to reflect my evolving vision and audience. This included updating my logo, website, and marketing materials. The new brand identity was more polished and professional, which helped attract high-end clients and gallery opportunities. I often had multiple versions of my main logo, which I used for different segments of my business. For instance, I had an amazing logo for my business, which was at the forefront of my website, however, I also created and used rebranded versions of the same logo, that were each slightly different, that I used for my wineglass painting parties, and for my pet portrait painting parties.

Licensing and Collaborations

Licensing my artwork for use on products like clothing, home decor, and stationery provided a new revenue stream and increased brand visibility. Collaborating with brands and designers expanded my reach and introduced my work to new audiences. For example, a collaboration with a well-known home decor brand led to a series of limited-edition prints that sold out quickly. These connections were made often at my parties and in person.

Hosting Workshops and Events

Hosting workshops and events helped establish my brand as an authority in the art world. These events provided opportunities to share my knowledge, connect with other artists, and attract new clients. For instance, hosting an annual art retreat allowed me to engage deeply with participants and build lasting relationships. My monthly painting parties were essentially a huge social networking event every month. I had many clients that would come to every single party. They wanted to have every design for themselves. The best part was, they often brought new people with them every time. And every month there would be new guests as well, and them being able to speak with my followers that had already fallen in love with me and my art was a massive bonus in marketing and advertising. It's one thing to tell someone that you're great, but for them to hear it from the mouth of another client for themselves is worth more than gold in your business. Make room for these moments to occur. You won't be sorry.

Building a Sustainable Business Model

Sustainability is key to long-term success. Here's how I built a sustainable business model:

Financial Planning

Careful financial planning ensured that my business remained profitable and resilient. I created detailed budgets, tracked expenses, and reinvested profits into the business. This financial discipline allowed me to weather economic fluctuations and invest in growth opportunities. Make it a habit to always save a percentage of every check. I would actually divide everything in to a 50/30/20 rule. 50% would go to needs such as bills, groceries, transportation; the essentials and non-negotiables. 30% would be allocated for wants, and discretionary spending, such as dining out, entertainment, hobbies, vacations, and other non essential purchases. Then, 20% would be allocated strictly for savings and debt repayment. This can include contributions to an emergency fund, retirement accounts, investments, and paying off debts beyond the minimum payments.

Diversifying Income Streams

Diversifying income streams reduced financial risk and provided stability. In addition to selling original art and prints, I offered workshops, online courses, and consulting services. I also provided murals, and custom glassware, private lessons and parties, in addition to my monthly parties. This diversification ensured that I had multiple revenue streams, which protected my business from market downturns. I can't stress enough how important this is. There will rarely be a moment where all cylinders are firing at the same time. So, ensure you have many back up cylinders to keep you afloat when one or two most assuredly have downturns throughout the seasons. Expect problems, and plan for them, then eat them for breakfast.

Sustainable Practices

Adopting sustainable practices was not only environmentally responsible but also attracted eco-conscious clients. I used eco-friendly materials, minimized waste, and promoted sustainable art practices. This commitment to sustainability became a key aspect of my brand identity.

Personal Story: Navigating Challenges and Celebrating Milestones

Overcoming Setbacks

Every business faces setbacks, and mine was no exception. One significant challenge was when a major project fell through due to unforeseen circumstances. This setback was financially and emotionally draining, but it taught me the importance of resilience and adaptability. I refocused my efforts on smaller projects and gradually rebuilt my momentum.

Celebrating Milestones

Celebrating milestones kept me motivated and provided a sense of accomplishment. Whether it was reaching a sales target, hosting a successful exhibition, or receiving an award, each milestone was a testament to my hard work and dedication. For example, hosting my first solo exhibition in a renowned gallery was a significant milestone that boosted my confidence and credibility. Sharing all of your wins, big and small alike, on social media is critical to sustaining your online presence and following. They want to enjoy the ride with you every step of the way. Through the good and the bad. But especially the wins. You can even use the milestone moments to generate even more gains, by offering a creative contest or a game with your clients and social media following in celebration of a new milestone achievement. This a great way to build off of momentum and gain sales.

Staying Connected with My Passion

Amidst the business aspects, staying connected with my passion for art was essential. I regularly set aside time for personal projects and creative exploration. This balance ensured that my work remained inspired and fulfilling, which in turn resonated with my audience. And I would share my personal work online as well. Your followers will love this insight in to your personal life.

Future Goals and Vision

Looking to the future, I have set new goals to continue growing and evolving my business:

Expanding My Reach

I aim to expand my reach by exploring international markets and participating in global exhibitions. This involves networking with international galleries, building relationships with overseas clients, and leveraging online platforms to reach a global audience. I am currently working on ways to implement virtual painting parties and a subscription service. This will allow to residual income as well as expand my reach well beyond even just my country.

Innovating with Technology

Embracing new technologies like blockchain and NFTs (non-fungible tokens) will open up new opportunities in the digital art world. I plan to explore these technologies to create unique digital art pieces and reach tech-savvy collectors. This concept is very new to me, however I plan to dedicate time to really research and learn everything that I can in order to see ways I could implement this in to my art business.

Giving Back to the Community

Giving back to the community is an important aspect of my vision. I plan to establish a scholarship fund for aspiring artists, host free workshops for underprivileged communities, and collaborate with nonprofits to use art for social good. I have done many live painting events for charity and each time I have found myself rewarded well beyond my investment. This commitment to social responsibility will enhance your brand and make a positive impact on your community.

Conclusion of Chapter 11

Planning for continued growth and success involves setting long-term goals, staying adaptable, expanding your brand, building a sustainable business model, and navigating challenges with resilience. By maintaining a clear vision, embracing innovation, and staying true to your passion, you can ensure that your art business thrives for years to come.

Chapter 12: Conclusion and Final Thoughts

Reflecting on the Journey

As we reach the conclusion of "The Not So Starving Artist," it's important to reflect on the journey and the valuable lessons learned along the way. Building a successful art business is a challenging but rewarding endeavor. Here's a recap of the key steps and personal experiences that shaped my journey and can guide yours.

Starting with Passion and Determination

Every journey begins with a single step. My passion for art and determination to succeed were the driving forces behind my initial efforts. Despite numerous setbacks, such as not being able to attend Ringling College, I found alternative ways to pursue my dream. This passion and determination are essential for overcoming obstacles and staying motivated. Stumbling blocks, or stepping stones, remember?

When I couldn't attend Ringling College due to financial constraints, I didn't let this setback define my future. Instead, I used it as fuel to explore other opportunities and push forward. I remember thinking about Edison's quote, "I have not failed. I've just found 10,000 ways that won't work." This mindset helped me embrace failure as a stepping stone to success. TV shows and documentaries like, "The Men Who Built America," were very motivating and inspirational for me in instilling a business mindset with my art.

Building a Strong Foundation

The foundation of a successful art business lies in understanding your market, building a brand, and creating high-quality work. Early in my career, I focused on developing my skills, understanding my audience, and establishing a strong online presence. These foundational steps set the stage for future growth and success.

Embracing Failure and Learning from Setbacks

Failures and setbacks are inevitable, but they are also valuable learning experiences. From the dissolution of my initial partnership to navigating financial challenges, each setback taught me resilience and adaptability. Embracing failure as a catalyst for growth is crucial for long-term success.

When my partnership with my photographer friend fell apart, it felt like the end of my dreams. However, I picked myself up, got a job as a server, and dedicated all my free time to rebuilding my art business. I learned that "not trying is just another form of failure." This determination kept me moving forward even when the odds seemed against me.

Innovating and Adapting

Innovation and adaptability are key to staying relevant in a constantly changing market. I continuously explored new mediums, technologies, and business models to keep my work fresh and exciting. This willingness to adapt allowed me to reach new audiences and seize emerging opportunities.

For example, I developed wine glass painting parties and pet portrait events, which became significant sources of income. These innovative ideas came from thinking outside the box and recognizing that "things don't get better by chance, they get better with change."

Building Strong Relationships

Strong relationships with clients, collaborators, and the art community are vital for sustained success. Providing excellent customer service, following up with clients, and expanding my network helped build a loyal client base and opened up new opportunities. These relationships are the backbone of a thriving art business.

Maintaining Work-Life Balance

Balancing personal and professional life is essential for long-term well-being and productivity. Setting boundaries, prioritizing self-care, and scheduling regular breaks helped me maintain this balance. This approach not only improved my well-being but also enhanced my creativity and business performance.

Setting Long-term Goals and Planning for the Future

Setting clear, achievable long-term goals provided direction and motivation. Breaking these goals into actionable steps and continuously revisiting and adapting my plans ensured steady progress. Planning for the future, embracing innovation, and staying connected with my passion are crucial for continued growth and success.

Words of Encouragement

As you embark on or continue your journey to build a successful art business, remember that every artist's path is unique. Here are some words of encouragement based on my experiences:

Believe in Yourself

Self-belief is the foundation of success. Trust in your abilities, stay true to your vision, and don't let setbacks deter you. Your passion and creativity are powerful tools that can overcome any obstacle. Remember, "it only takes one time of getting it right to succeed."

Stay Resilient and Adaptable

Resilience and adaptability are essential traits for navigating the ups and downs of an art business. Embrace challenges as opportunities for growth and stay open to change. Your ability to adapt will set you apart and keep your business thriving.

Seek Support and Build Community

You don't have to navigate this journey alone. Seek support from friends, family, mentors, and fellow artists. Building a community of like-minded individuals will provide encouragement, inspiration, and valuable insights. I learned that "the relationship was important for my small business" and building strong connections is key.

Keep Learning and Innovating

The art world is constantly evolving, and continuous learning and innovation are key to staying relevant. Invest in your education, explore new mediums and technologies, and stay informed about industry trends. Your willingness to learn and innovate will drive your success.

Celebrate Your Achievements

Take time to celebrate your achievements, both big and small. Each milestone is a testament to your hard work and dedication. Celebrating your successes will keep you motivated and remind you of how far you've come.

Personal Story: A Glimpse into the Future

As I look to the future, I am excited about the possibilities and opportunities that lie ahead. Here are some of my future plans and aspirations:

Expanding My Reach

I aim to continue expanding my reach by exploring international markets and participating in global exhibitions. This involves networking with international galleries, building relationships with overseas clients, and leveraging online platforms to reach a global audience. My goal is to make my art accessible to people all over the world. This book is one of those ways I hope to help other aspiring artists achieve their dreams. I remember feeling alone and had no idea where to turn to in order to figure how to start my business. I was very daunting at time. I hope that I can be the help and inspiration for that new young artist that is wanting to find success amidst everyone around them saying that it is not possible.

Innovating with Technology

Embracing new technologies like blockchain and NFTs (non-fungible tokens) will open up new opportunities in the digital art world. I plan to explore these technologies to create unique digital art pieces and reach tech-savvy collectors. This innovation will keep my work at the forefront of the art industry.

Giving Back to the Community

Giving back to the community is an important aspect of my vision. I plan to establish a scholarship fund for aspiring artists, host free workshops for underprivileged communities, and collaborate with nonprofits to use art for social good. This commitment to social responsibility will enhance my brand and make a positive impact.

Continuing to Create and Inspire

At the heart of everything, my passion for creating and inspiring others remains. I will continue to explore new ideas, push the boundaries of my creativity, and share my journey with others. My hope is to inspire future generations of artists to pursue their dreams and build successful art businesses.

Final Thoughts

"The Not So Starving Artist" is more than just a guide; it's a testament to the possibilities that lie within each aspiring artist. By embracing your passion, building strong relationships, staying resilient, and continuously innovating, you can overcome the myth of the starving artist and achieve your dreams.

Thank you for joining me on this journey. I hope my experiences, insights, and strategies inspire and guide you as you build your own successful art business. Remember, the path to success is not always straightforward, but with determination and perseverance, you can create a thriving and fulfilling career as an artist.

Jayson Blondin is an accomplished artist and entrepreneur known for his innovative approach to the art business. After overcoming numerous challenges, Jayson built a thriving career and now shares his journey and insights through his writing. Connect with Jayson on social media and visit his website for more resources. See Author page at end of this book for links.

Acknowledgments

I would like to thank everyone who has supported me along the way – my family, friends, mentors, clients, and the art community. Your encouragement, feedback, and belief in my vision have been instrumental in my journey. This book is dedicated to you and to all the aspiring artists who dare to dream and work towards their goals.

About the Author

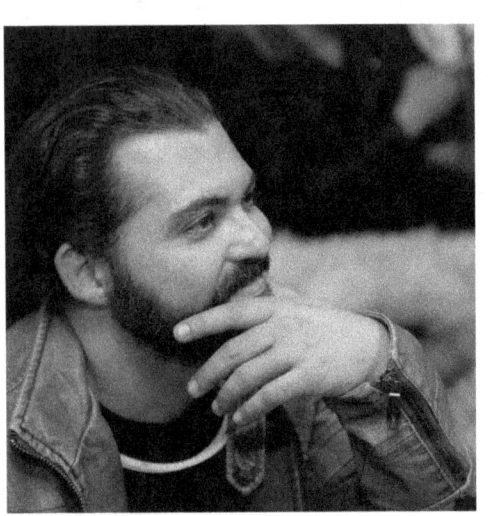

Jayson Blondin is an accomplished artist and entrepreneur known for blending creativity with business acumen. He founded Creative Synergy LLC, a thriving art business, after overcoming financial obstacles and personal challenges. Jayson is passionate about helping aspiring artists achieve their dreams and believes in the power of combining artistic passion with a solid business strategy. Follow Jayson on Facebook at JaysonBlondinArt and visit his website at www.JaysonBlondinArt.com for more tips, updates, and resources.

www.ingramcontent.com/pod-product-compliance
Lightning Source LLC
Chambersburg PA
CBHW050114230526
45470CB00004B/1824